LOL JOKES
PORTLAND

arcadia®
CHILDREN'S BOOKS

CRAIG YOE!

Published by Arcadia Children's Books
A Division of Arcadia Publishing
Charleston, SC
www.arcadiapublishing.com

First published 2021

Manufactured in the United States

ISBN 978-1-4671-9843-1

Library of Congress Control Number: 2021938358

All images used © Shutterstock.com; p.13 VECTOR FUN/
Shutterstock.com; pp. 14-15 Bob Pool/Shutterstock.com; p. 62 Leigh
Trail/Shutterstock.com; p. 74 Dee Browning/Shutterstock.com; p. 81
EQRoy/Shutterstock.com; p. 85 ARTYOORAN/
Shutterstock.com; pp. 92-93 Victoria Ditkovsky/Shutterstock.com.
Cover illustration: Craig Yoe
Design: Jessica Nevins

Craig Yoe has written a TON of kids'
joke books! Yoe has been a creative
director for Nickelodeon, Disney, and
Jim Henson at the Muppets. Raised
in the Midwest, he has lived from
New York to California and has six kids!

CONTENTS

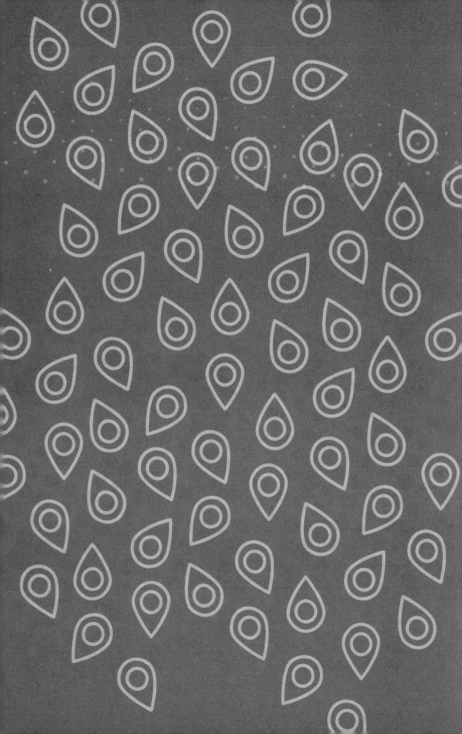

INSANE FACTOID

NOW, HERE'S A *SMALL* TIDBIT!

Guinness World Records has decreed that Mill Ends Park is the smallest park in the world— it measures only two feet across! Journalist Dick Fagen proposed the park for snail races and as a colony for **LEPRECHAUNS**!

IT WAS A TOSS-UP!

In 1842, the founders of Portland disagreed on what the city should be called. One proposed Boston, Oregon. The other came up with Portland, Oregon. Amazing but true: the name was decided by the toss of a coin! And I guess you know which one won!

9

FUN FACTOID

Trust me, Portland has SEVENTEEN BRIDGES!

**DOCTOR! DOCTOR!
I think I'm a
Stumptown bridge!**

What's come
over you?!

**Six cars, three
trucks, thirty-seven
cyclists, and an
electric scooter!**

St. Johns Bridge

Yo, wuss UP?! For Real! Portland has a vertical street!

Known as "**ELEVATOR STREET**," the Oregon City Municipal Elevator connects downtown Portland to the neighborhood of McLoughlin.

Why did the elevator go to the doctor?

It thought it was COMING DOWN WITH SOMETHING!

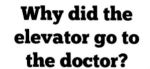

AN ELEPHANT
+ DARTH VADER
= AN ELE-VADER!

ELEPHANT:
I'M AFRAID OF ELEVATORS!

DARTH VADER:
YOU NEED TO TAKE *STEPS* TO
AVOID THEM!

A WHEEL-Y COOL FACTOID!
Portland boasts over 350 miles of bikeways! Stumptown is one of the most bike-friendly cities in the U.S.

A WHEEL-Y WEIRD FACTOID!
Portland hosts an official **WORST DAY OF THE YEAR** bike ride! Thousands of tough-minded Portlanders ride their bikes for miles in costume during this harsh winter event. It's been described as "Halloween in February!"

The annual Bridge Pedal event over the Fremont bridge

What's the hardest part about learning to ride a bike?

STOP IN THE NAME OF THE LAW!

at the Portland Police Museum!

You'll see bodacious badges, early arrest photos, records, and cool cop uniforms! But don't do anything wrong, or you'll get thrown in the old jail cell displayed there. (Not really.)

My son Donovan is a cop and we came up with these arresting police jokes for you:

What do you call a police officer in bed?

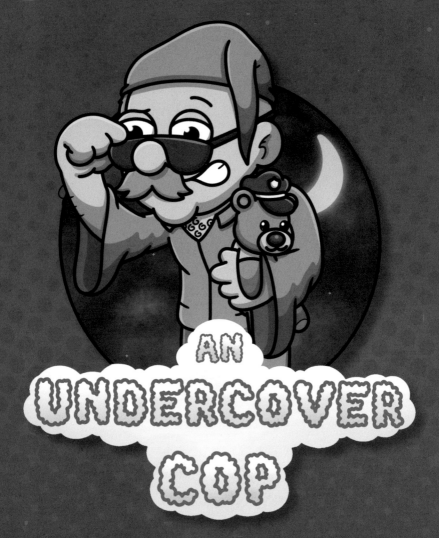

AN UNDERCOVER COP

Me: Did you read about the theft of over 100 wigs from Portland's Wigland Wig Store?

Donovan: Yep, the cops are **COMBING** the area!

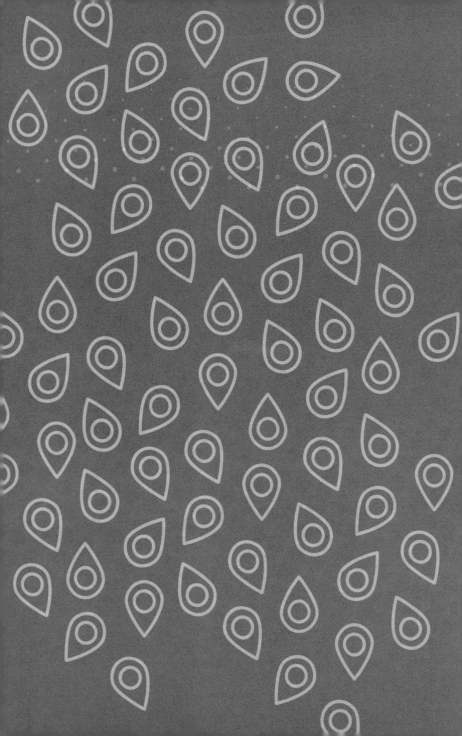

In Portland, it's **AGAINST THE LAW** to perform a wedding ceremony on an ice-skating rink!

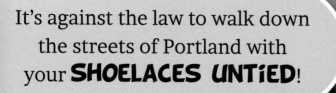

It's against the law to walk down the streets of Portland with your **SHOELACES UNTiED**!

Molly:

A man was just arrested for walking in Portland with untied shoelaces!

Steven:

Was it a *fell*-ony?

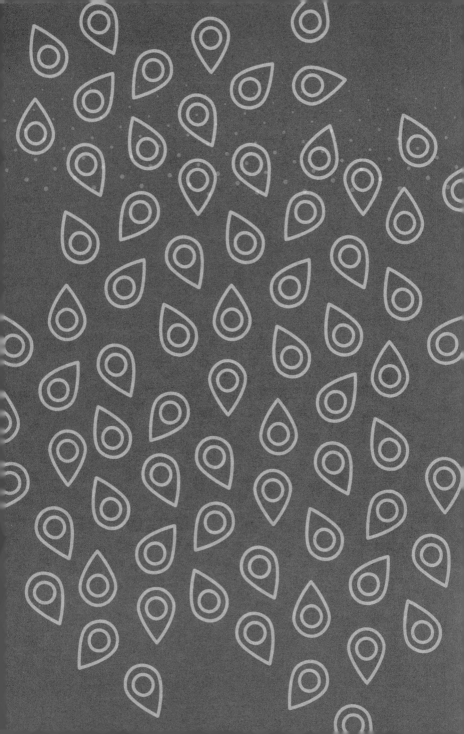

DO YOU *LAKE* THIS COLORFUL JOKE?!!

If you throw a red rock into Portland's Blue Lake, what does it become?

WET!

How do you get an elephant out of a tree?

SIT HIM ON A LEAF AND WAIT UNTIL FALL!

Forest Park

← WILDWOOD →
TRAIL

PORTLAND
PARKS & RECREATION

TREE-MENDOUS!

Forest Park is one of the largest urban forest reserves in the United States. It is home to 62 mammal species and 112 bird species!

YOU'RE GONNA "LAVA" THIS!

There's a mountain of volcanoes around Portland. In fact, Mount Tabor Park sits on an extinct volcano! Much of the park was formed by ancient lava—including the staircases and roads! Lava-out-loud with these yuks:

Where does a volcano wash its hands?

In the **LAVA**-tory!

What did the kid volcano call his mother?
Mag-MA!
What did the volca—
I KNOW THIS!
Hey! Don't int-ERUPT me!

ROWS AND ROWS AND

Portland is known as the City of Roses,
so I want to plant these rose jokes on you!

ROSE:
What did the Martian
say to the rosebush?

LILY:
I give up, what?

ROSE:
"Take me to your
WEEDER!"

ROSES ARE RED
VIOLETS ARE BLUE
I SAW A FACE LIKE YOURS
IN THE OREGON ZOO!

ROWS OF **ROSES!**

What did the bee say to the rose?

Wussup, **BUD**?!

GARDENER:
Hurry up and grow!

A ROSE:
I'm **PETAL**-ing
as fast as I can!

Roses in Washington Park

Multnomah Falls

PORTLAND HAS MAIN*STREAM* ATTRACTIONS: TRUE OR *FALLS*?

TRUE!

Portland has dozens of eye-popping waterfalls in the area, including the majestic Multnomah Falls.
Go with the flow by telling these waterfall jokes. They'll make your fam and friends *roar* with laughter!

What is the opposite of a waterfall?

A *FIRE FLY!*

Diana:

Did you hear about the H2O that tripped?

Malcolm:

Huh?

Diana:

Water*fell*.

Malcolm:

Oh, I fell for that one!

What did the waterfall say to the tourist?

"WATER you looking at?!"

FESTIVAL OF FUN!

Every year, Portland celebrates the Elephant Garlic Festival with a 10k run, music, a kids' play area, and a parade. (Elephant garlic is similar to regular garlic, only larger.) And to celebrate elephant garlic, here are my favorite elephant and garlic jokes.

Did you hear about the kid who was raised by a garlic clove?

Yeah, she was garlic *bred*!

41

How do you make an apple turnover?

YOU ROLL iT DOWN A HiLL!

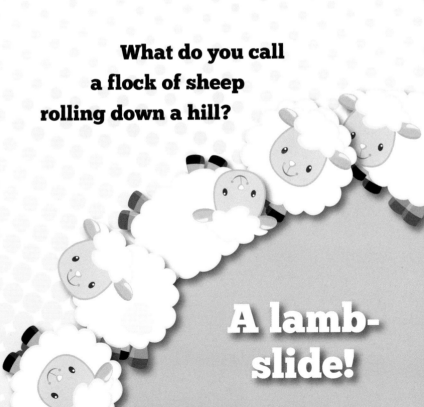

What do you call
a flock of sheep
rolling down a hill?

A lamb-
slide!

A FISHY JOKE

Herman

Portland is famous for fish. The most famous of all is Herman the Sturgeon, who you can see at the Sturgeon Viewing and Interpretive Center in nearby Bonneville.

What's the funniest fish?!

The **PiRANHAHAHAHA!**

I just broke my funny bone laughing so hard and now I have to see a **STURGEON**!

KEEP PORTLAND WEIRD DEPT.

Portland has a **WISHING TREE**! You can hang your wishes on its branches. People's wishes include wishes for world peace and more time to play video games! The tree can be found at 2954 NE 7th Ave.

TREE-MENDOUS!

What did the Wishing Tree grant the Portland Trail Blazer?

Three *swishes!*

RAIN, RAIN
IT NEVER GOES AWAY!

**Why does
Santa Claus
like Portland?**

**Because of the
RAIN, DEAR!**

**What does a Portland
rain cloud wear
under its raincoat?**

THUNDER-WEAR!

What kind of bear likes all the rain in Stumptown?

A *DRIZZLY* BEAR!

Yep, in Portland it rains cats and dogs—and I just stepped in a poodle!

MOUNTAINS

Why can't Mt. Hood and Mt. Bachelor play hide and seek?

Mt. Hood

OF MIRTH!

Because they always **PEAK**!

Mt. Bachelor

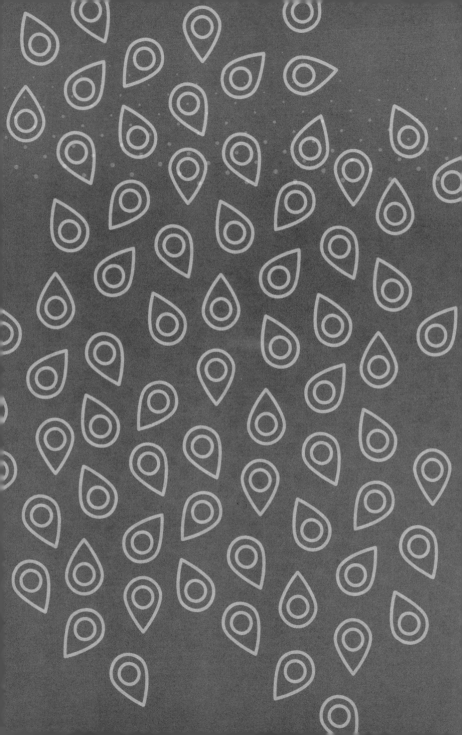

It's been said that in the spring, you could **WATERSKI** in downtown Portland in the morning, **SNOWBOARD** on Mount Hood at noon, and in the early evening, you could **SURF** in Seaside!

ALL THIS IN ONE DAY, YO!

Here are three LOLs about this fun factoid . . .

A joke for you to tell in the morning:

Why don't cowboys waterski in Portland?

BECAUSE THEIR HORSES WOULD DROWN!

A joke for you to tell in the afternoon:

What were the snowboarder's last words?

"DUDE, WATCH THIS!!!"

A joke for you to tell in the evening:

What kind of school does a surfer go to?

A BOARDING SCHOOL!

RUNNING

Portland is the home of **NiKE'S** and **ADiDAS'S** American operations! Let me **RUN** these jokes by you that I heard at Portland's Helium Comedy Club:

My favorite running shoes are retiring. Their soles aren't into it anymore, but they had a **GOOD RUN!**

So, I bought a new pair of **RUNNiNG** shoes the other day— let me know if you see them!

57

What's made of rubber and cloth, is a foot long, and sounds like a sneeze?

A SHOE!

Is it raining in Portland again or did you just sneeze?

Why didn't Cinderella make the Portland Thorns Team?

She ran away from the ball!

Why was the Trail Blazers' court wet?

The team **DRiBBLED** all over it!

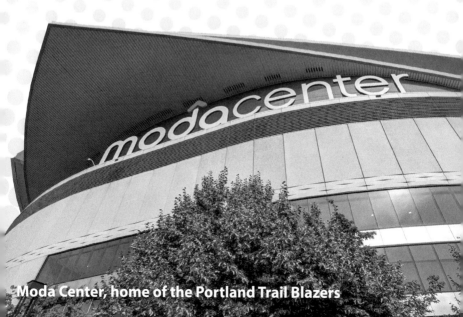

Moda Center, home of the Portland Trail Blazers

Why can't the Portland Trail Blazers go on vacation?

It's illegal to travel!

Do you know what the enforcer on the Winterhawks does?

Yes, of course!

Just checking!

What did the skeleton drive to the Winterhawks' game?

A Zam-BONE-y!

What do a Winterhawks player and a magician have in common?

THEY BOTH DO HAT TRICKS!

Did you hear about the guy who tried out for the Naughty Dogs (in the National Professional Paintball League)?

He got in with **FLYING COLORS**!

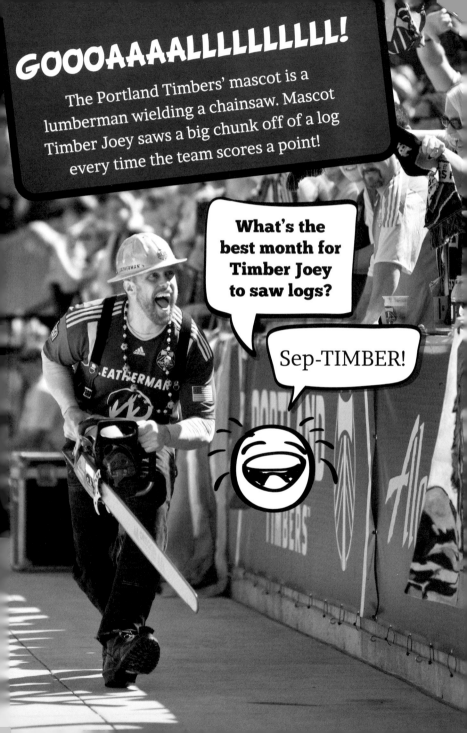

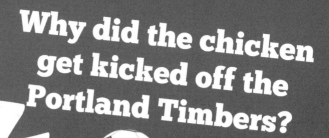

Why did the chicken get kicked off the Portland Timbers?

For **FOWL** play!

What position did the zombie play on the Portland Timbers?

Ghoulie!

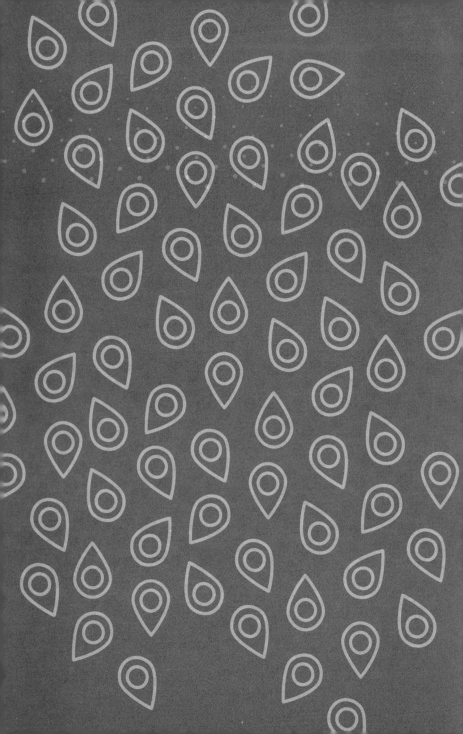

PARANORMAL JOKES

UN-*BOOOOO*-LIEVEABLE, BUT TRUE!

Some say that Oregon has the most ghost towns of any state in the U.S! To fête that fearful fact, here are some jokes to lift your *spirits*!

OMG! UFO LOLs!

Mulder:

What did the alien say to the *LOL Jokes: Portland* book?

Scully:

"Take me to your reader!"

Just 40 minutes southwest of Portland is McMinnville's UFO Festival: Three days of UFO fun! The festival is out of this world with a parade, live music, and an alien costume contest.

What did the aliens in the UFO message to Saturn?

How does a visitor from outer space put their baby to sleep?

They **ROCKET**!

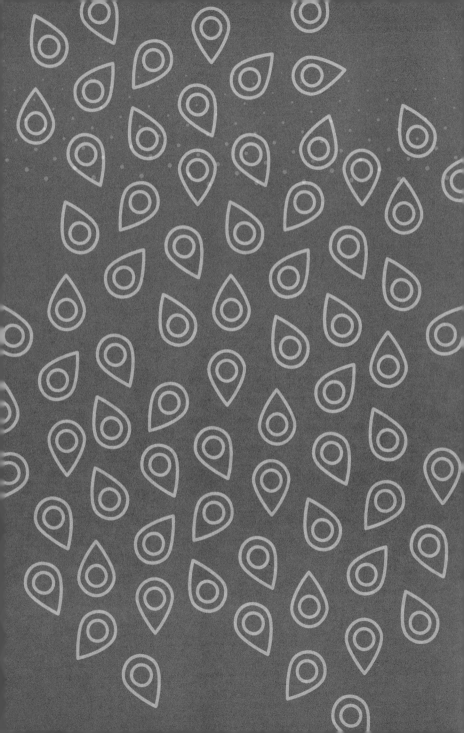

BIG NEWS AND SOME BIG LAFFS!

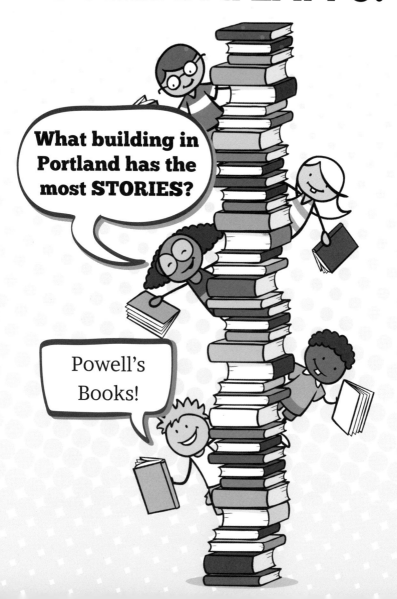

FUN FACTOID

It's a fact! Powell's is the largest independent bookstore on the planet. It has approximately ONE MILLION BOOKS—that's a lot of STORIES—in a lot of books! YAY BOOKS!

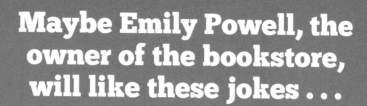

Maybe Emily Powell, the owner of the bookstore, will like these jokes . . .

How do you catch a school of fish?

With **BOOK**worms!

Where do Powell's one million books sleep?

Under their covers!

What's Bigfoot's favorite book?

Hairy Potter!

A LITTLE LIGHT HUMOR!

What Powell's is to books Sunlan Lighting is to lightbulbs! Tourists from all over the world come to bask in its glow and see the wacky window displays masterminded by the owner, known as the Lightbulb Lady!

Sulan customer:
I need two-watt bulbs.

Lightbulb Lady:
For *watt*?

Sunlan customer:
That'll be fine! Wrap 'em up!

The Portland Art Museum is the **LARGEST** art museum in Oregon— and one of the oldest in the U.S.!

Portland Art Museum

Tourist: Can we take pictures?

Museum Guard: Oh, no! The paintings have to stay **ON THE WALLS**!

How do chimpanzees go down the stairs?

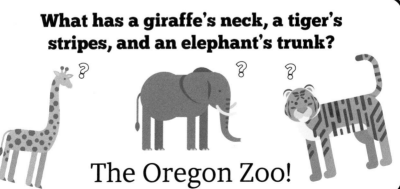

GIVE PEACE A CHANCE!

The beautiful, awe-inspiring and fun Portland Japanese Garden says on their website that it was "Born out of a hope that the experience of peace can contribute to a long-lasting peace. Portland Japanese Garden is a place of inclusivity, anti-racism, and cultural understanding."

Portland Japanese Garden

DO THE SIMPSONS REALLY LIVE IN PORTLAND?

The creator of **The Simpsons**, Matt Groening, was born and raised in Portland.

FUN FACTOID

Groening named many of the characters of his popular TV show after streets in Portland!

FLANDERS ST.

• **NED FLANDERS** was named after Flanders Street!

• Class bully **KEARNY** comes from NW Kearny Street!

• Groening named **MAYOR QUIMBY** after Quimby Street! Vote Quimby!

• Two Portland streets, Montgomery and Burnside, make up Homer's boss's name: **MONTGOMERY BURNS**! EX-cellent!

• There's NW Lovejoy Street that gave **REVEREND LOVEJOY** his moniker!

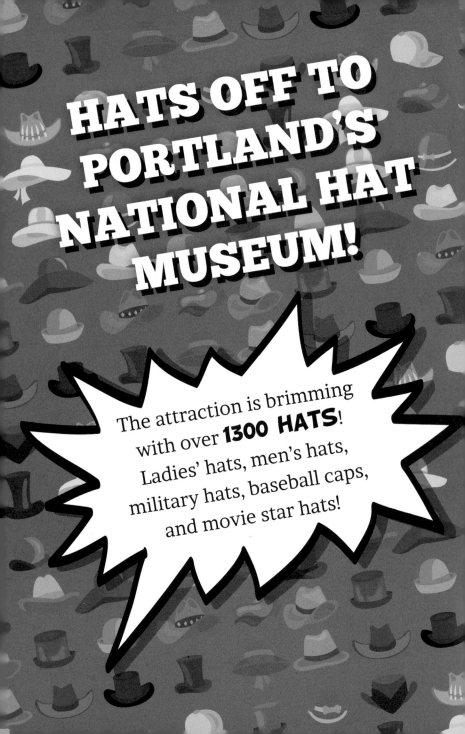

HATS OFF TO PORTLAND'S NATIONAL HAT MUSEUM!

The attraction is brimming with over **1300 HATS**! Ladies' hats, men's hats, military hats, baseball caps, and movie star hats!

95